PRAISE FOR
BEYOND PM TRAINING

Effective project management is the lifeblood of successful AEC firms, and in this essential guide, Anthony Fasano—an experienced engineering project manager dedicated to helping others thrive—provides a clear, practical methodology to build a customizable PM ecosystem for your team or firm. With a step-by-step approach designed to improve project success and profitability, this book will help you empower your team members to excel while delivering tremendous value to your company's bottom line. A must read to help your people and company succeed.

Michael J. Carragher, P.E.
President and CEO of VHB

Beyond PM Training is a must-read for anyone leading complex AEC projects and managing large teams. Anthony Fasano provides a clear roadmap for developing project managers beyond technical skills—fostering leadership, adaptability, and trust-based environments that are essential for successful project delivery. This book offers actionable insights that help leaders not only train project managers but cultivate a resilient, people-centered project management ecosystem that drives long-term success.

Kabri Lehrman-Schmid
Project Superintendent, Hensel Phelps

Unlock the key to building a truly effective project management ecosystem with *Beyond PM Training*. This insightful guide goes beyond the basics, providing a strategic approach to creating sustainable project management success.

Discover the importance of **clear role definitions, consistent processes, and intentional development**—the essential pillars of any high-performing team. With a focus on practical implementation and continuous growth, this book offers invaluable insights for firms and professionals looking to elevate their project management practices.

Joey Hudnall, P.E.
CEO of Neel-Schaffer, Inc.

In his book *Beyond PM Training: How to Build a Scalable AEC Project Management Ecosystem*, Anthony Fasano provides a guide for AEC firms on how to build a thriving and sustainable AEC Project Management Ecosystem™. He presents ideas that are way more advanced and effective than just typical "Project Management Training" or "Bootcamp." His approach is holistic and can thoughtfully be customized to the AEC firms' specific needs and where they are on their journey. Whether your AEC firm is just beginning, or has been in existence for decades I believe you will find this book useful and chockfull of tools and ideas that will be helpful to you. This book is a fantastic read, and the information within it is practical and based on Anthony's own experience and what he and his team have learned by helping many AEC firms along the way. I highly recommend this book.

Michael A. Shamma, P.E.
New York Metro Executive at TYLin

When project managers lead the members of a project team—rather than just manage a process—they unlock the true value that a project can deliver. Project managers become a linchpin for projects, a critical component in delivering an exceptional client experience while also ensuring team members are meaningfully engaged in their work. The framework discussed in this book is a great starting point to build the necessary mindset and skillsets for project managers within an organization.

Lynn Browning, P.E., PMP
Project Management Director, Henderson Engineers

The author of *Beyond PM Training: How to Build a Scalable AEC Project Management Ecosystem* emphasizes that effective project management is essential for the sustainable growth of AEC firms. The book advocates for a comprehensive PM development strategy that goes beyond traditional training, incorporating clear role definitions, continuous development, standardized tools, and efficient onboarding processes. By creating a project management office (PMO) and building a robust PM ecosystem, firms can ensure consistent project delivery and long-term success. The book highlights the importance of continuous improvement, networking, and maintaining both technical and leadership skills to keep PMs agile and competitive. A must-read for AEC executives seeking to drive sustainable growth in their organizations!

Rizwan A. Siddiqi, P.E.
President & CEO, EBA Engineering, Inc.

Project Management, at its core, is the combination of technical knowledge, communication, and leadership. While all are important, the successful combination of these skills varies greatly depending on the individual's development and maturity as a Project Manager, as Anthony Fasano stresses in *Beyond PM Training*. Like any endeavor, these skills require consistent training and exercise to develop, maintain, and grow. Fasano brings to light the responsibility that we as leaders owe our employees: the investment in development opportunities if we expect them to grow and deliver impactful results for our organization in such a competitive marketplace.

Ed Overholt, P.E., PMP
Vice President of Operations | Campos Fabrication, LLC

In his book, Anthony Fasano has presented solid ideas on how to improve project management in our firms. We work on projects of all sizes and complexities. Projects today are much more than scope, schedule, and fee. This book will be a valuable resource for improving your project management practices.

David A. DeLizza, P.E.
President & CEO, Pennoni

As someone who has transitioned into leadership in the AEC industry in the past few years, I found *Beyond PM Training: How to Build a Scalable AEC Project Management Ecosystem* to be incredibly insightful and practical. This book offers fresh, actionable strategies that go beyond traditional training, helping to build a robust project management ecosystem. It's an essential read for anyone looking to develop high-performing teams, achieve consistent project success, and obtain sustainable growth.

K. James Taylor, Jr., P.E.
Co-Host of The Civil Engineering Podcast, Associate Vice President at Verdantas

Sustainable growth in AEC firms isn't just about winning projects—it's about executing them effectively. This book delivers a proven roadmap for developing project managers into true leaders who drive profitability, efficiency, and consistency. A must-read for AEC executives committed to building a high-performing project management culture that attracts top talent and secures long-term success.

Richard A. Negri, P.E.
AEC PM, Principal at Geoterra Engineering & Construction Consultants

The concept of the PM Ecosystem is spot on. Preparing a project manager for their job is much more than just providing 'training'. Anthony's book outlines the foundation to building this Ecosystem in a way that's easy to understand. It's a lot of effort towards putting the appropriate processes, policies, procedures, and people in the right places, but the benefits can lead to better, more profitable projects, professional project managers, and increased retention.

Monique Mitchum, PMP
Assistant VP, GFT

BEYOND PM TRAINING

How to Build a Scalable
AEC Project Management Ecosystem

ANTHONY FASANO, P.E., AEC PM

Edited by Ella Rice & Michelle Cochran
AEC PM Ecosystem™ cover image by Elloise Ollave
Chapter illustrations by Anum Khan
Book Design by James Woosley, FreeAgentPress.com

ISBN: 979-8-9990797-0-1 (hardcover)
ISBN: 979-8-9990797-1-8 (paperback)
ISBN: 979-8-9990797-2-5 (e-book)

CONTENTS

FOREWORD

I N THE RAPIDLY EVOLVING landscape of the Architecture, Engineering, and Construction (AEC) industry, project management stands as a cornerstone for sustainable growth and success. As we navigate through an era marked by technological advancements and heightened competition, the ability to manage projects effectively is not merely a skill but a necessity. This book serves as a comprehensive guide to building a robust AEC Project Management Ecosystem™— a framework designed to transform traditional project management practices into a dynamic, scalable, and sustainable process.

Over the course of my career, I have seen firsthand the importance of effective project management at the "pointy end" of project delivery. When an effective project manager (PM) is at the helm, the project delivery team is organized and focused, the client is generally satisfied, and the project key performance indicators tend to sit within the limits.

Unsurprisingly, with a misaligned PM calling the shots, the project goes off the rails. What I've come to learn is that effective project managers in today's AEC industry are generally on-the-job success stories. They may hold a certification and may have additional training, but they learn as they go by doing the work. This book will illuminate this key point for you—that training must be considered as development, with an emphasis on continuous growth and adaptation—i.e., learning by doing, then adjusting and growing.

The level of competition in today's AEC industry requires company leadership to spend time ensuring they have established a properly defined project management framework. Your company's livelihood is one, or a few, poorly delivered projects away from financial challenge. As I have had the opportunity to sit in both the operations and delivery, and the growth and sales sides of AEC businesses—your sales team can't outsell bad project delivery!

Anthony presents a central theme in this book which highlights the importance of a well-defined project management (PM) ecosystem. He has done an excellent job of outlining an approach that, if considered, adjusted, and applied to a company's existing framework, I think can help greatly in mitigating a myriad of risks that come from an ineffective or inadequate PM program.

Anthony also touches on the importance of onboarding and mentoring, a highly important consideration in every company! Small and large AEC firms alike need to have equally effective programs in place to ensure that your new team members receive the right amount of integration into the business. Otherwise, you may find yourself making investments in their skills, only to see them working for your competitor before you know what happened.

Central to the book's philosophy is the idea that project management development is an ongoing journey, not a destination. It requires commitment, adaptability, and a willingness to embrace change. This is a concept that is highly important for both company leaders and individuals to embrace, since one's effectiveness as a PM doesn't stop with receipt of the PMP or some other credential. The insights shared in this book are drawn from years of experience and collaboration with AEC firms across the globe. They reflect a deep understanding of the industry's challenges and opportunities, offering practical strategies that can be implemented at any stage of an organization's development. As you embark on the journey of building your AEC PM Ecosystem™, remember that the ultimate goal is to create an environment where project managers can thrive. By investing in their development, you are investing in the future of your organization. The lessons and strategies outlined in this book will not only enhance your project management capabilities but also contribute to the sustainable growth and success of your firm.

In closing, I invite you to embrace the challenge of transforming your project management practices. Let this book be your guide and inspiration as you build a scalable, resilient, and effective PM ecosystem. The future of your organization depends on it, and the rewards of your efforts will be profound and lasting.

Christian Knutson, CEng, P.E., PgMP, PMP
Experienced Program Manager

THE KEY TO SUSTAINABLE GROWTH

FAILING INFRASTRUCTURE, ADVANCING TECHNOLOGY, contaminated water in our water system, among many other global challenges, have made the civil infrastructure industry a good (and profitable) place for professionals and businesses to reside for the last twenty years. This positive business climate looks to continue for the foreseeable future. Firms can prosper in this environment if, and only if, they can figure out how to grow in a sustainable way; where they can hire, develop, and retain enough professionals to do the work, profitably. This is easier said than done.

While business has been good for architecture, engineering, and construction (AEC) firms, recruiting as well as developing and retaining staff has been harder than ever, and it's not getting any easier.

Not only is the market uber-competitive, but there aren't enough engineering professionals to begin with in the United States, which is why AEC firms need to stand out to attract them. On top of that, even if AEC firms find talent, the next battle becomes retaining them, as other firms in need of staff are aggressively recruiting them. It's a vicious cycle.

An analysis of Bureau of Labor Statistics (BLS) data prepared by Boston Consulting Group showed that the U.S. alone will need about 400,000 new engineers and that nearly one in three engineering roles will remain unfilled each year through 2030.[1] More work, more competition, fewer people to do it. It doesn't take an engineer to see that it is a losing equation.

However, I believe that I have found the key to sustainable development for AEC firms: **effective project management.**

Figure 1: PM Success Cycle (Engineering Management Institute, 2025)

1   Machine Design. Salary & Career Survey: Mechanical Engineering Talent is in Short Supply https://www.machinedesign.com/community/article/55249303/salary-career-survey-mechanical-engineering-talent-is-in-short-supply

Coffee shops sell coffee, landscaping companies sell landscaping services, AEC firms sell their time, but they sell it through the delivery of projects. The more successfully a project is delivered, the more profit it generates, the more profit, the more funds a firm has available to invest in recruiting and developing their teams. That may sound like a very rudimentary philosophy, but it really is that simple.

So, how does an AEC firm execute effective project management? Here's a hint, it requires a lot more than sending some of your project managers (PMs) to a PM bootcamp every so often.

WHY PM TRAINING ISN'T ENOUGH

For most of my career as a civil engineer, I have always cringed when I heard the words "PM Training." "Why?" you might ask.... Early in my career I was employed by a well-known engineering consulting firm, and when it came time for me to make that heralded transition from engineer to project manager, they sent me to PM training. Unfortunately, the PM training ended up being an overwhelming and highly stressful experience.

The experience involved me being sent away for a few days to a hotel to go through training with a group of other AEC professionals that I had never met before. The training consisted of two long days, where I received a barrage of project management information in a binder that we went through hour by hour (even though it felt like day by day). Talk about information overload!

The content that I received during this training was excellent, but the prospect of trying to digest it all in one sitting was daunting. To make matters even worse, I was sent home with this binder, which I was supposed to reference in all my future project management efforts. The reality was, I would get back to my office, put the binder on my shelf, get swallowed up by my project responsibilities, and never open that binder again. Now, there may be project managers that refer to the binder (or maybe a PDF these days) from time to time, but very few professionals have the time to truly digest the content and put it into practice.

Fast forward to several years later, I had left my career as a civil engineer and started the Engineering Management Institute (EMI) with the goal of helping AEC organizations, like my previous employer, develop their professionals into strong project managers and leaders. I knew from my own experience that to help these firms achieve real, sustainable growth, we would need to offer more than traditional PM training.

Before I go further, I want to define the phrase sustainable growth since I will use it throughout this book. The American Business Magazine Inc. gives the definition of sustainable growth as "the realistically attainable growth that a company could maintain without running into problems." Directly related to sustainable growth is the term sustainable growth rate, usually abbreviated as SGR, which the Magazine refers to as "the maximum growth rate that a company can sustain without having to increase financial leverage."[2]

To that end, there are two lessons I have learned over the past 15 years of helping many AEC firms develop stronger project managers and leaders, and ultimately achieve sustainable growth. First, effective project management is the absolute key to sustainable growth for AEC firms, and I'll explain why in the coming paragraphs. Second, PM training is not enough. If an AEC organization wants to be world class, and grow sustainably, they must develop and maintain a project management (PM) ecosystem.

---

2   Prysmian Magazine. INSIGHT https://www.prysmian.com/en/insight/sustainability/sustainable-growth-what-does-it-mean

ENTER THE AEC PM ECOSYSTEM™

Effective project management requires that your organization addresses **ALL** facets of project management. This includes clear job titles, role descriptions, and clear career pathways for your project managers. You'll need a world class development program (not just training) focused on PM and people leadership skills, strategically built around the 5 PM process groups: Initiating, Planning, Executing, Monitoring and Controlling, and Closing. You must provide your PMs with the proper tools and templates as well as the right PM software. You'll have to get good at onboarding PMs, which might include mentoring, and maybe eventually develop a Project Management Office (PMO). All these components together make up your PM ecosystem, which will ultimately serve as a well-oiled machine to help you develop world class project managers while breeding consistency in your PM efforts companywide.

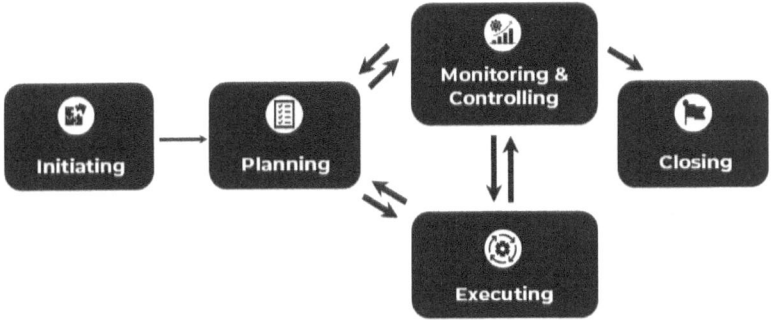

Figure 2: Five Process Groups
(Project Management Institute, 2025)

Now, the idea of an entire PM ecosystem might be overwhelming to you, especially if your firm is small to mid-sized, or simply hasn't developed many of these ecosystem components yet. To avoid feeling overwhelmed, as you read through this book, I want you to take on the following mindset of building out your PM ecosystem.

In Figure 3, I present to you the AEC PM Ecosystem™. Each component plays a role in a healthy PM ecosystem. I've grouped these components into four phases: PM Pillars, PM Development, PM Utilities, and PM Support. **The good news is that you do not need all 8 components to be successful in your project management efforts, and you DO NOT need to develop them in order.**

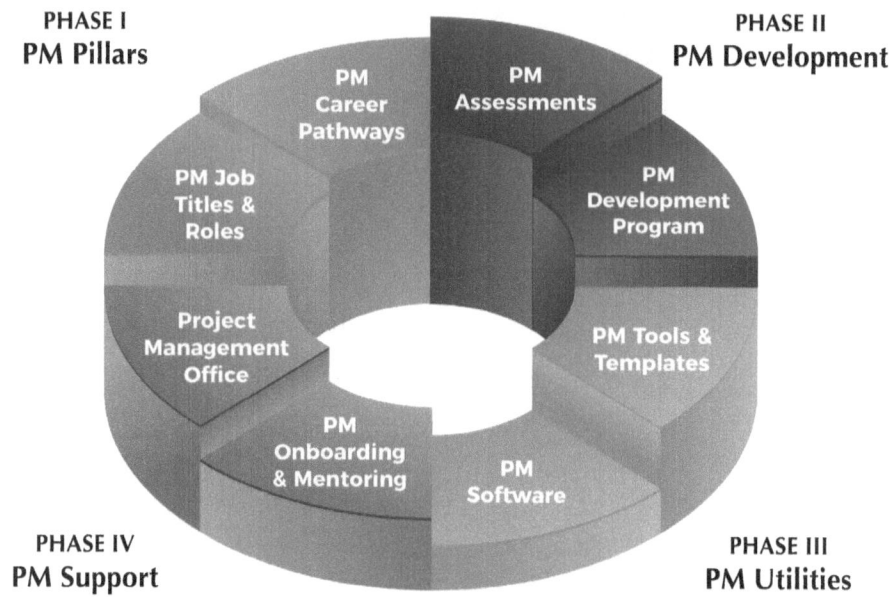

PHASE I
PM Pillars

PHASE II
PM Development

PHASE IV
PM Support

PHASE III
PM Utilities

Figure 3: AEC PM Ecosystem™
(Engineering Management Institute, 2025)

If you were starting from scratch, you would approach the phases in order, but that rarely happens. For example, several of our clients will focus on PM Development (Phase II) first by assessing and building a development program for their PMs, and then will work on job titles, role descriptions, and career paths (Phase I). Another example might be a firm who has used a PM software for some time (Phase III) but has yet to build a PM Development Program (Phase II).

In the following pages, I will outline strategies that your firm can use to build out each of these PM ecosystem components. For years, my firm has worked with both public and private AEC organizations to help them build PM ecosystems, and from that experience, I've learned what works in PM development, and what is wasting your time and money. I've conducted hundreds of interviews with PMs through our podcast network and our custom PM learning and development program design process, so I understand **exactly what your PMs need**, and I am ready to share it with you.

I am excited to take you on this journey beyond PM training to find the key to sustainable growth for AEC firms: effective project management through building a scalable AEC PM Ecosystem™, piece by piece. While developing this ecosystem won't be easy at times, it could be worth millions of dollars to your AEC firm, so I promise you, giving it your attention is worth your time

PHASE I

PM Pillars

PM
Career
Pathways

PM
Job Titles &
Roles

PHASE IV

PM Support

PHASE II
PM Development

PHASE III
PM Utilities

IDENTITY CRISIS
Who or What is an AEC PM?

HOW MANY PROJECT MANAGERS work for your organization? Yes, I am asking you to answer that question. Can you?

Most AEC organizations that we work with can't. They usually say something like, "Well, I will need a few days to try to figure out how I can answer that question."

Really? Your company is built around delivering projects, your project managers are responsible for executing these projects on time and within budget, and you don't know who your PMs are? As one of our PM instructors, Ann Tomalavage, always says, "Project managers are the cashflow engines of all AEC firms."

Seriously, you don't know how many PMs work for your organization?

Think about the ramifications of this. If you don't know who your PMs are, you can't evaluate their performance regularly, you can't train them properly, and you certainly can't determine whether or not you have enough PMs to manage your backlog of projects.

I would equate this to a baseball team that isn't quite sure how many pitchers they have on their roster. "Well, we know we have a lot of players that can throw the ball, so we'll figure out how to make it through all our games," the team manager might say.

That's not how building an AEC organization works. You can't hope that you have enough project managers, and that they have the skills, tools, and templates needed to succeed. In fact, in this book, I will make a case that building your PM ecosystem should be one of the most important actions your organization takes. You must know each of your PMs, their strengths and weaknesses, and how you can help them to be the absolute best PMs that they can be. The future of your organization depends on it.

WHY AEC FIRMS CAN'T FIGURE THIS OUT

Why is it so hard for most AEC firms to answer the question of how many PMs they currently employ? Simple. The position of a project manager within an AEC firm is poorly defined. In most AEC organizations that we've worked with, the term "project manager" is seen as "something one does in addition to their primary job function." For example, Megan might be a civil engineer, but she also manages projects, or Sanjiv might be a geotechnical department manager, but he also manages 20 projects.

This is a major problem, and something I like to refer to as the *PM Identity Crisis*. Your firm needs to clearly define what a project manager is in your organization so you know who your project managers are, only then can you focus on developing them appropriately.

Going back to my baseball analogy. A pitcher in baseball is defined by Dictionary.com as, "the player in baseball who throws the ball to the opposing batter."[3] Well, the shortstop can certainly

---

3   "Pitcher." Dictionary.com. 2025. https://www.dictionary.com/browse/pitcher (15 February 2025).

throw or "pitch" a ball from the mound to the batter, but is he or she a pitcher? No, and consequently, he or she doesn't need the same strength or mechanics training that a pitcher receives.

Not all your engineers or architects are or should be project managers, and if you can't clearly identify which ones are, achieving sustainable growth is going to be difficult. Just as winning a championship would be difficult for a baseball team who asks their shortstop to pitch.

START WITH A CLEAR DEFINITION

No matter the size of your organization, if you haven't clearly defined the role of a Project Manager, stop right now, drop everything and do it.

I know, you are wondering, how? You can start by going through the following list of questions with your leadership. While going through this exercise, know that when you are finished, you are going to want to clearly be able to answer the question: **How many PMs do we currently have within our organization?**

INITIAL QUESTIONS:

1. Is "Project Manager" a primary job title within our organization or is it a secondary title (or role) that people have (or do) in addition to their primary job title (i.e. civil engineer)? Answer either: primary or secondary.

2. Are there people in our organization that solely manage projects, or is project management something that people always do in addition to many other things? Answer either: people solely manage projects or people manage projects in addition to other tasks.

For most organizations, the answers to these questions will conclude that project management is NOT the sole title of most professionals, and yes, project management is something they do in addition to their primary job. If that is true of your organization, then proceed with the following questions. If it's not true for your firm, then you can stop here, because you already know how many PMs you employ, strictly by title.

Questions to Ask if Your Answers Revealed that Project Management is Secondary

- ✓ Is there an easy way for you to identify everyone in your organization who manages projects?
- ✓ If not, could you create a formal secondary title of Project Manager (i.e., Anthony Fasano, P.E., AEC PM, Civil Engineer/Project Manager)?
- ✓ Is there a way you can create a career path dedicated to project management that can serve as an overlay to other career paths? For example, I might be a Civil Engineer II | Junior PM.
- ✓ On that Project Management Career Path, can you create various career steps (i.e., Junior PM, Deputy PM, Project Manager, Senior PM, etc.)?

Solving the PM Identity Crisis

Once you have answered these questions, you will have the basis for identifying every person in your organization who manages projects, as well as the framework for a PM career path. Most importantly, you will be able to answer the question: **How many project managers do you have in your firm?** I cannot understate this. This is absolutely critical.

Solving the PM identity crisis will help you to achieve the following:

1. Provide a clear career path for project managers within your organization. This matters because most AEC professionals covet the title Project Manager more than anything else in their careers.

2. You will be able to better develop your project managers by identifying them and their experience as a PM using the career progression strategy. This includes building or finding PM development programs to match each stage of the career progression.

3. Building on the two previous points, your PMs will be able to better manage and deliver projects, which is how your organization survives (and thrives).

If you want to build a scalable PM ecosystem, a critical first step is defining the role of a project manager within your organization and being able to create a list of **all** of your project managers. Without this information, it will be difficult to budget the proper resources to build out each phase of your PM ecosystem.

PHASE II

PHASE I
PM Pillars

PHASE IV
PM Support

PM DEVE

PM
ssessments

PM Development

PM
Development
Program

PM Utilities

CHAPTER 2

NOT ALL PMs ARE CREATED EQUAL

OST AEC FIRMS MAKE a critical mistake when it comes to developing PMs. They assume that the progression and skill level for PMs at different stages of their careers are the same. This is a dangerous assumption. A project manager with three years of experience could be better suited than a much more experienced PM to manage a certain project based on their background, experience, and current skill levels. **Not all PMs are created equal.**

I believe there is a good reason that many AEC firms and professionals make this assumption. Professional engineers at these firms follow a very logical licensing progression. Most professional engineers take what's called the Fundamentals of Engineering (FE) exam towards the end of their undergraduate studies. They then work for approximately 4 years (depending on the state they reside in) and then take the second exam, the Principles and Practice of

Engineering (PE) exam and if they pass, they become a licensed professional engineer.

You're either a PE or you're not. You can either sign and seal plans and specifications, or you can't. Unfortunately, as I described in the previous chapter, the role of a PM in the AEC world is much more vague than that.

In most organizations, future project managers start out as team members working on projects and reporting to project managers. As they progress and take on more responsibilities, their PM or their organization may earmark them as a future PM. From that point on, their development hinges directly on that organization's process for developing PMs, and as I mentioned before and will mention again throughout this book, let's hope it's not solely sending them to an all-day bootcamp and then throwing them to the wolves.

WHY YOU SHOULD ASSESS YOUR PROJECT MANAGERS

If you want to develop your PMs the right way, you need to understand the developmental needs of **each** of them. You can't make blanket assumptions about the skill levels of all soon-to-be PMs versus all 3-year PMs, you need data to inform your development efforts.

I strongly recommend that the first step in PM development be to assess the skill levels and development needs of your PMs through any of the following actions:

- Create and administer a survey with very specific questions around their development to ALL project managers.
- Utilize internal or external industry assessment tools (i.e., the AEC PM Behaviors Assessment) to assess your PMs skills across the five PM Process Groups.

- Conduct interviews with various PMs of different experience levels and disciplines within your organization.

The clarity you gain from these actions will help to ensure you build your PM ecosystem in a way that best supports your PMs. Once you've taken these actions and have collected data specific to your PMs, you can chart out a PM development program or strategy that will speak specifically to YOUR project managers—not generic industry standards. Yes, you should create your own project management standards that should be followed companywide.

We have conducted hundreds of interviews with AEC project managers, and the thing we hear most often is, "I wish my company would give me more than a generic PM training, it is such a waste of my valuable time."

I'd like to go a little deeper on each of these actions, to provide you with some steps you can take to successfully collect the data that will give you an accurate cumulative skill profile of your project managers. This profile can be used to ensure the PM Development phase of your PM ecosystem is highly relevant to and productive for your organization.

SURVEYING YOUR PROJECT MANAGERS

If you plan to survey your PMs, or retain a firm like EMI to do so, there are a few recommendations I will provide you with to ensure you get the data that will best serve your PM development efforts.

Firstly, ensure that you segment all the PMs taking the survey by their experience managing projects, NOT career experience. There might be two professionals, one with five years of experience and one with twenty, but they both may only have two years of project management experience—that's an important distinction.

Once you've segmented them by PM experience, then ask each group questions that pertain to their experience level. For example, you might ask soon-to-be or beginner PMs very topical questions about the PM process groups, whereas your questions on these topics geared towards experienced PMs may be much more detailed.

Ask a mix of simple and open-ended questions to allow them to really share their thoughts. Simple questions might be true or false, or yes or no questions. For example, "Do you feel the firm has provided sufficient PM training?"

Please note, I am using the word training because that's unfortunately what most AEC professionals are used to hearing, although I would prefer to use the word, "development." The power in open-ended questions is that they cannot be answered with a simple yes or no. For example, "How can our firm improve our PM development efforts?"

While the simple questions help to build momentum for survey takers and can provide some good cumulative data, more value will come from the thoughts shared through the answers to the open-ended questions. These answers will likely help to influence your PM development plan and program, and ensure you are not making the dangerous assumption that all PMs are equal in their development stages.

Lastly, give a deadline for participants to complete the survey and let them know that their answers WILL influence their future development as PMs. People typically don't like surveys UNLESS the surveys are going to help them in a measurable way.

HOW TO ASSESS YOUR PROJECT MANAGERS

Formally assessing your PMs using an assessment tool can be just as helpful as a survey, if not more. There are many different assessment tools out there, so how will you know which is the best for your organization? Again, keep in mind here, we are talking about project management, so ideally you would want to assess your professionals on the skills associated with project management and the 5 PM process groups.

When we started building custom PM programs for firms years ago, we would encourage them to allow us to incorporate any assessment tools that they were using into their PM development programs. One can't develop as a PM, even if they go through a great program, unless they can identify some of the key areas where they need to develop personally.

Most of our clients were utilizing proven personality or skills-based assessments like the Myers-Briggs, DiSC, or StrengthsFinder. These are all excellent tools, in fact, we use some of them at EMI internally, but they tell us nothing about one's ability to manage projects successfully.

After a few years of designing PM development programs, we were introduced to the Harrison Assessment, a behavioral assessment that measures one's strengths and weaknesses related to the *behaviors* required to perform one's job role, not their personality or skills. The Harrison Library has over 200 job competencies, so, for example, if I took the assessment under the job competency of a civil engineer, I would get a report on my strengths and weaknesses related to the behaviors necessary to be successful as a civil engineer based on previous civil engineers who took the assessment.

After discovering the power of the Harrison Assessment, we decided to collaborate with a company called Talent Matters, a managing partner of the Harrison Assessment, to develop a competency in the Harrison Library specifically for AEC Project Managers. To accurately develop the competency, we gave the assessment to 100 AEC project managers AND had their managers rate each of them in each of the five PM process groups: initiating, planning, executing, monitoring & controlling, and closing. Now, the AEC PM Behaviors Assessment allows firms to utilize their PMs' strengths and weaknesses as they relate to relevant job skills, both individually and across their organization.

Just imagine if in one chart you could see how competent ALL of your PMs were through behavioral traits across the 5 PM process groups. For example, if your PMs are generally good at monitoring projects, but poor in closing projects, where do you think you should focus more of your PM development efforts? You can be much more strategic and productive in your development efforts.

Here's one example of how helpful this information can be to a PM from an article by Trusted Coach. Trusted Coach says, because the AEC PM Behaviors Assessment utilizes the Harrison Assessment competencies library, it utilizes the Paradox Theory when considering the relationship between traits. Trusted Coach continues, "For example, Diplomatic and Frank are a paradoxical pair of traits included in the Harrison library. Frank is the Dynamic aspect and Diplomatic is the Gentle aspect of communication...." A person who can be both frank and diplomatic at the same time will manifest the FORTHRIGHT DIPLOMACY trait and be an effective communicator in resolving everyday work relationship issues. On the other hand, a person who tends to be very frank but lacking in diplomacy will be quite BLUNT. A person who tends to be very diplomatic and at the same time is extremely lacking in frankness will tend to be EVASIVE."[4]

All that being said, if you plan to assess your PMs, do your best to use a tool that can give you data on their skill levels RELATED to project management. You may have an internal tool you can use, or maybe you use a third-party tool like the AEC PM Behaviors

---

[4] Harrison Assessments Theory. (2015). Trusted Coach. https://www. trustedcoach.com/wp-content/uploads/2015/01/HA-Theory.pdf

Assessment, but whatever you use, be sure you can tie the results back to project management.

The last thing I will say about assessments is that you should have a clear plan for your PMs to use the results of each assessment. Personality assessments are great for awareness purposes. If I know my personality or communication work style as a PM or a leader, it can inform the way I engage with other people. However, my personality type will likely change very little, if at all, over my career.

With behavioral assessments, once I understand my behaviors, I can improve the most relevant ones through development efforts. For example, with many of our PM development clients, we start by giving the AEC PM Behaviors assessment to their PMs. Next, we use the data to ensure we design the program around that organization's biggest needs. Then prior to the program starting, we debrief the participants on their specific assessment results, so that they know the behaviors that they need to focus on improving. This allows them to really maximize the development program and use the content to focus on specific behaviors they need to improve, increasing the return-on-investment of the program, creating a win-win for both the PMs and their organizations.

So, assessments can be tremendously helpful, as long as you select the right ones for your team and have a plan for how you will utilize the results.

INTERVIEWING YOUR PMs

No matter how many surveys or assessments you run, or how much hard data you collect, it is always worth the time to talk with your project managers. Whether this is done through informal discussions or formal interviews, you can learn so much about how PMs feel they are being supported by your organization and where they see their current skill levels.

When we build custom PM development programs for firms, we always ask to interview a cross section of professionals within each organization including project team members, junior PMs, senior PMs, and even the accounting team that works with PMs all the way up to the CFO. Project Management is such an important aspect of AEC organizations; we want to learn as much as we can about it in that organization.

We also interview professionals both in groups, and individually. Doing this allows you to ask different types of questions and quickly assess how project management practices vary across a firm in different disciplines, sectors, or geographic regions.

You might consider having a third-party conduct anonymous interviews if you think you would get more honest feedback from those interviewees.

One of our goals when we are building a custom PM program, is to try to help our clients build more consistency in their PM efforts across the organization. The interviews can uncover some areas where consistency can immediately be improved based on thoughts and case studies from interviews.

One last recommendation on interviews. If the interviewees, and your HR team members, are comfortable with you recording the interviews, do so. You can then take all the recordings and use AI programs to summarize the data and present patterns that can be extremely helpful in creating an effective PM development process.

At EMI, we host a podcast called The AEC PM Podcast, a free resource that can help you identify the right questions that you can ask your PMs. We share some of the questions we use in our client PM interviews in the PM Resource Pack which can be downloaded at PMResourcePack.com.

So, as you think about PM development in your organization, remember that not all PMs are created equal, and the more data you can collect, specific to your PMs' skill levels, the more success-ful your development efforts will be.

CHAPTER 3

THINK "PM DEVELOPMENT" NOT "PM TRAINING"

THE WORD "TRAINING" HAS become a scary word to AEC professionals. Training is either something that most AEC professionals want to avoid like the plague, or they want to do it quickly, meaning, get in and get out. For example, an AEC professional might think, "My training for this month is to log into my company's 'university,' watch one webinar, check it off, get my professional development hour (PDH), and then get back to more important billable activities." THIS MENTALITY MUST CHANGE IN THE AEC INDUSTRY! And this change will be driven by leaders like you.

This mentality has been cultivated over years of billable professionals trying to stay 95% billable, or utilized, and being allowed very little time for training or development activities. In fact, many companies say, "Do training on your own time." Yeah right.

Outside of working 40 to 50 hours per week for you, and my family and other personal obligations, who has time to train "on their own time?"

News flash: if you keep telling your employees to do training "on their own time," they will go work for a company that allows them to develop themselves as part of their jobs.

PM BOOTCAMPS RARELY WORK— INFORMATION OVERLOAD!

When I started my career working for a top Engineering News-Record (ENR) consulting firm, they used to send me to PM Bootcamp. Just hearing the word *bootcamp* now gives me terrible flashbacks. Don't get me wrong, the content in these bootcamps was stellar, the instructors were above average, but the problem was **too much** information. You've likely heard of the term, "Drinking from a fire hose," well that's what the bootcamp felt like. For two straight days, in a hotel, away from my family, I learned every detail of the 5 PM process groups. Then, I went back to work on Monday morning, opened up my email inbox, and never looked at the PM Bootcamp binder or any of the content again.

So, my company paid thousands of dollars for me to go to this one-off training event, and realistically I probably implemented less than 5% of what I learned. However, they were able to check the box off next to PM Training for Anthony Fasano, for whatever that's worth (not much in my opinion). They also lost money on me not being billable for two days plus travel expenses. Ouch. Talk about a losing proposition.

It's events like this bootcamp, and one-off PDH webinars that are given by PDH companies or online "universities" that have created this stigma around the word "training." Most AEC professionals think of training as a one-time event where they get some information on a topic of importance. Whether they can digest and use that information to improve their performance or not is where "training" typically fails.

MAKING THE CHANGE FROM TRAINING TO DEVELOPMENT

A few years ago, at the Engineering Management Institute, we made a decision to replace the word *training* with *development.* Before I give you our rationale behind this decision, let me share with you the definitions of these two terms:

> *Train means to undergo discipline and instruction, drill, etc.*[5]

> *Develop means to bring out the capabilities or possibilities of; bring to a more advanced or effective state.*[6]

At EMI, we felt that "training" indicated a one-off event or the action of one getting the information. Whereas "development" covers not only the event where the individual gets the information, but how they use it over time to develop their skills or themselves.

This was a big decision for us because our clients and prospective clients always referred to PM programs as "PM Training," or "PM Bootcamp," not PM Development. However, we made the change globally, and haven't looked back since.

When we build programs for our clients, we literally call them *Company Name* PM Development Program. This sends an immediate message to participants that this is not a one and done occurrence. In fact, we usually build multi-tier programs that consist of

5   "Train." Dictionary.com. 2025. https://www.dictionary.com/browse/train (15 February 2025).

6   "Develop." Dictionary.com. 2025. https://www.dictionary.com/browse/develop (15 February 2025).

foundations and advanced courses given to participants over an extended period of time.

Most of the custom PM Development Programs that we create are built around the philosophy of Spaced Repetition, which is a learning technique that involves reviewing material at increasing intervals to improve long-term retention. Typically, our courses are a series of shorter virtual or in-person sessions spaced out over time.

We also challenge participants to complete practical activities in-between sessions. For example, maybe they need to practice active listening in their next client meeting or create a risk register for an active project. This is the absolute best way to learn, hands-on. At EMI we've also created an industry recognized certification.

Our AEC PM Certification provides goal-oriented learning, giving participants more than just a certificate or logo to hang on their wall. AEC PM Certification recipients have access to our PM Assist™ service, which includes micro-learning reinforcement videos and webinars, and other exclusive PM content. The point is that reinforcing what your PMs have learned is essential to effective project management, which we'll get into later.

I also want to mention that a lot of AEC professionals will say something to the effect of, "In-person training is much better than virtual training." That is a very subjective statement and not necessarily true. While there are some benefits to in-person training, like the ability to role-play, relationship building and team building, from a learning perspective, small amounts of new information can be easier to digest, even if delivered virtually, rather than getting all the information at once.

Think about what would have a greater effect on your professional development, information overload once a year, or information opportunities throughout the year with built in time to review the previous content.

DEVELOPMENT WITHOUT REINFORCEMENT IS JUST TRAINING

I can't stress enough how critical reinforcement of the concepts is AFTER the development program is completed. This is where most PM development efforts fail miserably. As I mentioned earlier, when I finished the PM Bootcamp, I literally took the binder they gave me, put it on my shelf and never looked at it again. That can't happen if you want your PM Development Program to be effective. There MUST be follow up activities with program participants for a substantial amount of time after the program is presented to make sure they are truly building these skills. Again, *development* not "training."

Stop right now, and ask yourself, "Are we training our PMs or are we developing them?"

We design all of our programs based on a philosophy called The Six Disciplines of Breakthrough Learning. This is a framework developed by Roy V. H. Pollock, Andrew Mck. Jefferson, and Calhoun W. Wick. You can see these steps in Figure 2 and the process is detailed in a book entitled *The Six Disciplines of Breakthrough Learning: How to Turn Training into Business Results* (Wiley 2015).

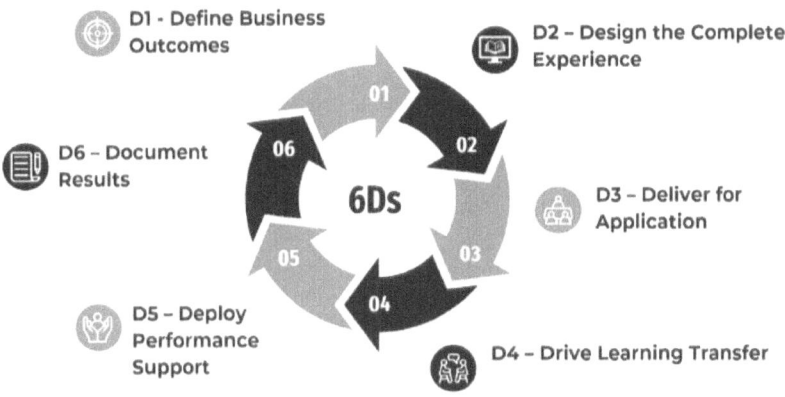

Figure 4: The Six Disciplines of Breakthrough Learning
(Pollock, Mck. Jefferson, Wick, 2015)

The key to this philosophy is the reinforcement after the development program, which very few AEC firms provide. Now, I want to challenge you to go against the AEC industry status quo and rename and redesign your "training programs" to be more development focused. I also want to challenge you to incorporate programs that use Spaced Repetition as opposed to one-time training events. The return on investment (ROI) of your programs will increase dramatically if you make these changes. Your PM Development Program will be the backbone of your AEC PM Ecosystem™.

It's time for our industry to choose out with the old (PM Training and PM Bootcamp) and in with the new (PM Development). An easy way to teach this to your team is to use the mantra, "Training NOT Development."

CHAPTER 4

PM BOOTCAMP ALONE DOESN'T WORK
You Need a Project Management Development Strategy

O VER THE PAST FIFTEEN years, I've had the chance to talk to hundreds of AEC leaders through many different avenues including conferences, sales calls, podcast interviews, and client strategy meetings. What I've discovered through these conversations is that most AEC organizations share the same strategy for PM development, which they explain as, "We send a few of our project managers to a bootcamp or off-site training program once per year."

That's it? When the success of your entire organization is predicated on delivering projects profitably, does that sound like an effective, high ROI approach to developing the people who are directly responsible for delivering those projects? The answer is a resounding NO!

In fact, I spoke to someone recently who oversaw project management at an AEC firm of 3,000 employees and asked them about their approach to developing PMs. This organization has about 400 project managers in total, and their strategy for developing them was to bring 40 of them together in person, once per year, and conduct a PM "training" that consisted of a few days of information overload, before they sent them back to their busy project laden professional lives.

Most AEC organizations today are growing at a rate of at least 10% per year, if not more. So, if you do the math, the firm I am referring to is probably adding 10 to 20 project managers to their company each year, and they are only training (not developing) 40 per year. That is not a sustainable approach to developing PMs companywide, and certainly won't contribute to a scalable PM ecosystem. If you work as a PM in this company, you would be lucky to receive some type of training every 5 years. That is not a place I would want to develop my career as a project manager.

It's imperative that you have a strategy for PM Development, as PM training is not enough. Let's talk about your PM development planning. Anything worth doing in life requires two actions. Number one, create a strategy for what you want to accomplish, and number two, execute the strategy by putting it into action. I want to help you take these two actions related to developing PMs in your organization.

ACTION #1—CREATE A SOUND PM DEVELOPMENT STRATEGY

The first step your organization should take is to develop a strategy for how you plan to **consistently** develop your project managers in ALL areas that they need developing. This, at a minimum, should include development on people leadership skills, project management skills (scoping, scheduling, budgeting, etc.), and technology (tools, software, etc.).

To create your PM Development Strategy (PMDS), I recommend following these seven steps:

1. Analyze Your Current Situation
2. Define the Objective
3. Identify Key Stakeholders
4. Set Priorities
5. Develop the Strategic Plan
6. Anticipate Risks and Challenges
7. Communicate the Strategy

#1 Analyze Your Current Situation

To create a strategy to improve your approach to PM development, you must look at how you currently develop project managers. Gather as much data as you can about current PM performance and any training or development that you provide. You might look at items like utilization, project write-offs, percentage of clients that come back for repeat work, and any other data that would indicate how your PMs have performed/developed over time.

One potential way to do this is to conduct a SWOT analysis, which is a process that you would go through to identify internal strengths and weaknesses, as well as any external opportunities and threats related to the development of your project managers. SWOT analysis is often traced back to the 1960s and the work of Albert Humphrey, a management consultant who was part of the Stanford Research Institute (SRI). Many organizations use a SWOT analysis to identify and evaluate their internal strengths and weaknesses, as well as external opportunities and threats.

The SWOT Sections	
Strengths • We've previously provided development programs to our PMs • We have PM software	**Weaknesses** • We are deficient in PM tools and templates • We are not currently providing PM development programs
Threats • We may lose PMs due to lack of PM programs and tools • Project profitability may suffer	**Opportunity** • Improved PM development programs and onboarding processes may yield better project delivery and PM retention

Figure 5: SWOT Quadrants Sample
(Engineering Management Institute, 2025)

Lastly, you should consider any industry standards or trends, and see if you can understand how your competitors are developing their PMs. Prospective clients often contact us and say something to the effect of, "We saw that one of our competitors certified their PMs with your AEC PM certification, we want to certify our PMs." If you know how your competitors are developing their PMs, there's no need to reinvent the wheel.

#2 Define the Objective

In this step, you must clearly outline what you want to achieve with your PMDS. Is there a certain standard you are striving for with your project managers? Is there a minimum amount of education you want them to receive annually? Is there a certain number of basic tools that you want to equip your project managers with? Do you want your PMs to achieve a specific certification (i.e., AEC PM)?

Set measurable goals around your objectives that can be evaluated periodically when you execute this strategy. For example, you may want to decrease project write-offs or variances by 10% next year. Ultimately, you should create a simple scorecard with key performance indicators that can be measured to ensure you are executing your strategy long-term.

Lastly, be sure that your objective is in alignment with your organization's mission, vision, or values, or it may not get the traction you desire. Don't gloss over the last sentence. Our values at EMI are Give, Guide, and Grow. We look to unlock growth in others and ourselves. As soon as any of our team members feel that an initiative or a party we are working with is not aligned with that, we stop and discuss it. Failure to do this will erode your culture.

#3 Identify Key Stakeholders

Like any good project manager, you must identify the key stakeholders. Stakeholders are the individuals or parties that can impact your organization's ability to develop your PMs, positively or negatively. Some of the stakeholders might include the PMs themselves, their managers, or your financial leaders who will have to approve the budget, etc.

Not only will you need to identify your stakeholders, but you will need to clearly explain to them the business outcomes of your PMDS. If they can see the value it will bring, it will be easier to gain their buy-in and support. Remember, they are likely going to be asking themselves, "What's in it for me?"

For example, you might show them how profits will increase, or write-offs will decrease based on improved project management efforts. This will likely get their attention.

This is a critical, but often overlooked step, in creating a strategy because without stakeholder buy-in, it will be very difficult to execute your strategy successfully.

#4 Set Priorities

In this step, you should identify the most impactful actions that you can take to execute your strategy and achieve the objective of developing your project managers.

I am a huge fan of the Pareto Principle, also known as the *80/20 Rule,* which says that 80% of one's success on any initiative comes from 20% of the actions taken. In this step, you are identifying the 20% of your actions during execution that will drive 80% of your success.

For example, a huge step in PM development will be getting approval for a certain number of "unbillable" hours, which are hours where your PMs can be engaged in training and development activities. Company leadership will need to feel confident in the proposed return-on-investment before signing off on a large number of unbillable hours. Part of this step should also be to consider what resources (time, budget, personnel) will be needed to execute your strategy.

An 80/20 Chart[7] is a great way to set priorities for your PMDS. You can populate the chart when you initially outline your strategy and then update it periodically.

---

7   Koch, Richard. *Living the 80/20 Way: Work Less, Worry Less, Succeed More, Enjoy More.* UNKNO, 2004.

Figure 6: 80/20 Chart
(*Living the 80/20 Way*, Koch, 2014)

#5 Develop the Strategic Plan

Please do not confuse this step with the strategic plan for your organization, because most AEC organizations do have a companywide
strategic plan. While not the same, the strategic plan for PM development should contribute to the companywide strategic plan. For
example, one of the components of your companywide strategic
plan might be to reduce write-offs, and developing your PMs' scoping and budgeting skills would contribute to that strategic initiative.

In this step, you are creating a plan for how you will break
down your PMDS into actionable steps. You will want to clearly
define who is responsible and accountable for each of these steps
and set deadlines and milestones to be able to track each.

Essentially you are creating a work breakdown structure (which
we teach in our PM development programs) for how you will execute your strategy. The Project Management Institute defines a

work breakdown structure (WBS) as a product-oriented "family tree" of project components that organizes and defines the total scope of the project. Each descending level represents an increasingly detailed definition of a project component. Project components may be products or services.[8] Just like we teach the PMs in our certification courses, a well-developed WBS will ensure that you achieve your project milestones.

#6 Anticipate Risks and Challenges

One of the final steps in developing your PMDS will be to identify any risks and challenges that you may face in executing your strategy. You might even consider developing a risk register, which is a tool PMs typically use to identify and score their risks on projects to determine which are the most threatening.

Your biggest obstacle will be getting approval for a certain number of hours that each PM can engage in PM development (training, mentoring, etc.) because every hour they spend on development activities, they are not billing a project. However, successful organizations understand that by investing in development, their billable hours will be more productive and their projects more profitable.

Once you identify the risks, then you should develop a plan that you can use to deal with or minimize each risk and create contingency plans should risks be unavoidable.

#7 Communicate the Strategy

Your final step in developing your PMDS should be to communicate the vision for your PMDS with the key stakeholders or decision makers who will be critical to the execution.

---

8   A Guide to the Project Management Body of Knowledge (PMBOK), Exposure Draft (especially Chapter 5). September 1994. Project Management Institute, Upper Darby, PA.

This is your opportunity to start to gain buy-in from your stakeholders and ensure they understand their role and how the project will impact the organization positively in the long-term.

I know this seems like a lot of steps, but without a sound strategy it will be difficult to create an effective PMDS. To help you with this, we have created a PMDS checklist which is included in the PM Resource Pack that you can download at PMResourcePack.com.

ACTION #2—EXECUTE YOUR PROJECT MANAGEMENT DEVELOPMENT STRATEGY

Congratulations! You have successfully developed your Project Management Development Strategy™ (PMDS), a critical step in Phase II of your ecosystem development, now it's time to execute it. Like many things, this is easier said than done. I want to give you three steps that you can take to execute on your PMDS.

#1 Implement the Strategy

To implement your strategy, you will simply follow the plan that you outlined when you created your PMDS. However, you must remember to put extra emphasis on the most impactful action items. Remember, 20% of your actions will likely drive 80% of your success.

You must also monitor your progress regularly. Just like project management on AEC projects, we need to ensure that our project stays on schedule and is hitting all the key milestones. To do that, ensure that you have a simple scorecard with your key performance indicators (KPIs) and monitor them weekly.

At EMI, we use simple spreadsheets that allow our team members to simply indicate "Yes" or "No" each week as to whether they were able to work on a certain goal and provide a one sentence status update. If it's not easy to monitor progress, people won't do it, including you!

#2 Evaluate and Adjust

As you are monitoring your progress through your scorecard, you should be adjusting your approach as needed. For example, if your Board of Directors didn't review your PM Development Program budget when they were supposed to, follow up with them. Seek feedback from your stakeholders regularly and incorporate their feedback into your approach, again modifying as necessary.

The bottom line is that you must continually measure progress and adapt as needed. Challenges will arise (remember you planned on them when you created your strategy), and now, during execution, you must make the proper adjustments to overcome them.

#3 Celebrate Success and Document Lessons Learned

It's important to celebrate success throughout the execution phase, not just at the end of the project. If you do receive budget approval to run a development program for 50 project managers, celebrate it. Let your stakeholders know that a huge milestone on the project was achieved, in large part due to their contribution. This will keep people engaged and excited about the project and build momentum to carry you through to the finish line.

Lastly, both during the project execution and after completion be sure to document lessons learned. Doing so will ensure you can improve your process for the next big initiative. When we teach project managers how to document lessons learned after their projects, we recommend they ask three questions:
- What worked well?
- What could we do better?
- What changes will we make based on what we learned?

The last question is key, because it forces you to outline real actions that will be taken to improve your process going forward. It is said that Albert Einstein stated, "The definition of insanity is doing the same thing over and over and expecting a different result." Please avoid insanity by documenting lessons learned!

I hope I have helped you to understand through this chapter that sending your PMs periodically to a PM bootcamp is not enough to truly develop them and instill consistent project management practices.

You need an effective Project Management Development Strategy™ that can be executed companywide, and now you know the steps needed to create yours. To help you with this, we have created a PMDS checklist as part of the PM Resource Pack that you can download at PMResourcePack.com.

PHASE III

PHASE I
PM Pillars

PHASE IV
PM Support

PHASE II
PM Development

PM Tools & Templates

PM Software

PHASE III
PM Utilities

CHAPTER 5

ALL OVER THE MAP
PM Tools, Templates, Processes and Software (Including Artificial Intelligence)

WHEN **AEC ORGANIZATIONS REACH** out to us for assistance with their project management development efforts, they often lead with comments like, "Our company needs help with processes and tools to manage projects with more consistency."

Typically, AEC organizations are all over the map when it comes to the PM processes and tools they use. The way they manage projects seems to vary widely from one office or one discipline to another within their companies. Allowing your project managers to follow different processes and procedures, and use different tools and software, can make it very challenging for your organization to consistently deliver high-quality projects. Addressing these inconsistencies is an important step in building your scalable PM ecosystem.

WHY PROJECT MANAGEMENT IS SO VARIABLE WITHIN AEC ORGANIZATIONS

All AEC firms start with one person, or a few people, who decide they want to start and grow a small business. These people all have their own habits, tools, and processes when it comes to managing projects. One might have a checklist of items that they created to kick off a project effectively, while another one might have a spreadsheet they built to help track their projects' budgets.

As the organization grows, they hire more project managers, all of whom have their own project management styles, tools, and processes which I refer to as a *PM Personality*. This growth increases the variability in ways the organization manages projects, and unfortunately, the consistency of the final products.

As the company grows even more, different styles of project management are added to their profile, making it even more difficult to drive consistency. So, the company decides to invest in expensive PM software to help them manage their projects better. However, this strategy can sometimes make it worse, because only a certain number of PMs use the software, and of those who do, they don't learn it completely, and therefore don't reap all of its benefits. Ultimately, this step can often just add another variable into the equation, giving PMs more options of how to manage their projects.

If that wasn't enough variability, eventually, the company decides to acquire another company. The company they acquired uses a different PM software which probably wasn't fully adopted by their PMs either. Now they must decide which of the two software systems to adopt and try to convince half of their project managers to abandon the old software, which they invested time and energy to learn, and use the new one.

In this chapter, I would like to provide some guidelines for how your leadership can drive more consistency in your project management efforts. No, I am not going to recommend a certain software for multiple reasons. One being, it might be obsolete by the time you read this book, and secondly, I have often found it's not always that one software is better than another, it's more about selecting one, and going through an effective implementation process to ensure people know how to use it, which rarely happens.

The guidelines I am going to share with you are based on the development of a library of tools and templates we call the AEC PM Toolkit, which can be further customized to a firm's specific needs. It was a rigorous process where we examined tools and templates needed by our clients across each of the five PM process groups: initiating, planning, executing, monitoring and controlling, and closing.

#1 Assess Best Practices Among Your Current PM Population

Years ago, we were designing a custom PM development program for a large AEC firm, and as part of the process, we interviewed several of their project managers. Whenever we asked a question about how they conducted project resourcing activities, the response would always be something like, "Well, we don't really have a great process, but one of our PMs, Cindy, has developed a great spreadsheet that we use for resourcing."

After hearing Cindy's name mentioned over and over, we decided we should talk to Cindy. So, we did, and she explained her process. One of our recommendations to this firm was that they have Cindy teach resourcing as part of the program and they roll her spreadsheet tool out companywide to drive consistency and help people resource better.

The same thing happens with most firms we work with. These occurrences made it clear to me, that the best first step in driving more consistency, or what I like to refer to as the "lowest hanging fruit," is to assess what is currently working amongst your current PM population and see if there are some habits, tools, templates, or processes that you can better leverage companywide.

You can do this by sending a simple survey to all of your PMs to assess the current tools and processes they use on their projects. To help you with this, we've created a list of survey questions that you can use to survey your PMs in our PM Resource Pack which can be downloaded at PMResourcePack.com.

#2 Select Key Tools That Will Make It Easier for Your Project Managers to Succeed

When I refer to "tools" for the remainder of this chapter, I am referring to tools, templates, and software that a PM may use in managing projects. For example, we've developed templates to help our clients create better cost estimates and utilize earned value management for tracking their projects. We've also developed a scheduling template that helps to create a Gantt chart in Microsoft Excel.

Once you've identified the current portfolio of tools being utilized across your organization, you can assess them, and maybe compare them to prospective tools that you might add. This should be done with one goal in mind: **build a portfolio of tools that will make it easier for your project managers to succeed.**

For example, one of the areas that most AEC organizations struggle with is terrible execution of project kickoff meetings, or they don't hold kickoff meetings at all. A kickoff meeting is a meeting typically held at the beginning of a project that allows the project manager to review key project items with all stakeholders including, but not limited to, project goals, scope, schedule, budget, expectations for communication, etc. **The kickoff meeting is the most important meeting of any project.**

In assessing your PM tools companywide, you might decide to create one standard kickoff meeting agenda template to ensure that kickoff meetings are held and executed effectively. This one tool can drastically improve consistency across your organization's PM efforts. Just imagine the impact, if suddenly 20% or more of your projects now have kickoff meetings, or better executed kickoff meetings. This would be a gamechanger. This tool would make it easier for your PMs to be successful.

As part of this action item, it is important for you to lean on the *80/20 Rule* again and determine the 20% of the tools that will drive 80% of the success of your PMs. I used an example of a kickoff meeting agenda because across our AEC PM Toolkit clients this is one of our most popular templates, and one that often drives big results.

So, spend some time thinking about which tools will make it easier for your PMs to succeed, and implement the most impactful ones first. This will ensure that the PM Utility portion of your PM ecosystem is not only functional but practical as well.

#3 Be Flexible with Some of Your Rules for Tools

I have discussed the importance of driving consistency with tools across your organization in this chapter, however, there are instances where exceptions should be made. For example, if you have a project manager who has been working with a large public organization client and he or she has had success with a certain budgeting or invoicing template with this organization for years, it doesn't make sense to change it.

Some of our clients who are successful in project management do this really well. They establish guidelines for tools and templates, but they do allow some flexibility because they understand that projects in different disciplines or geographic locations may have different requirements whether those be code requirements or client preferences.

We can't ignore the fact that all projects and clients are different, and one size may not fit all. Let's revisit the example I used earlier about creating a kickoff meeting agenda. You might have to create various kickoff meeting agendas for different types of projects such as public, private, small, large, etc. You might even provide a simple baseline template and allow your PMs to modify it to suit their needs. At least by creating the base template, you are reinforcing the importance of holding a kickoff meeting, but still giving your PMs flexibility in how they execute it.

This last guideline on flexibility may seem insignificant, but it could be the most important part of driving more consistency. Your PMs will appreciate you providing tools that allow them to adjust to their specific project needs.

You may have heard of Agile Project Management from the Project Management Institute. It is defined as a methodology that involves breaking down a project into smaller, iterative cycles, allowing for continuous feedback and adaptation to changing requirements throughout the development process, with a focus on collaboration and delivering value early and often, typically used in software development.[9]

Agile project management is a perfect approach to identifying and integrating the right PM tools and templates into your PM efforts. You may have to ask some of your PMs to try out a new tool, and provide feedback, and then modify it accordingly, until it puts your PMs in the best position to succeed. **Be aggressive in your pursuit of consistency but be flexible with the tools you use to get there.**

---

9   Project Management Institute. (2021). A Guide to the Project
      Management Body of Knowledge (PMBOK® Guide)---Seventh Edition.
      Newtown Square, PA: Project Management Institute.

ARTIFICIAL INTELLIGENCE (AI) IN PROJECT MANAGEMENT

I would be remiss if I didn't mention artificial intelligence (AI) in this book, and this chapter is the place to do it. Merriam-Webster defines Artificial Intelligence as the capability of computer systems or algorithms to imitate intelligent human behavior.[10]

AI in project management is not something I can cover in this book because the topic is too broad, however, I will make two points based on what I have learned through working with our many AEC clients.

Number one, AI will be a major factor in how AEC organizations manage projects going forward. It has the potential to streamline and expedite project management and provide invaluable project management data that firms can use to drive the consistency I've talked about in this chapter.

However, my second point is a recommendation to take it slow with AI, maybe even take an agile approach. To some degree, AI in the AEC world is still a "wild, wild, west" atmosphere. There are so many new AI tools, some better than others, and most organizations don't know where to start. My recommendation is to start small by testing out one or two technologies with a small part of your employee population before a larger investment is made or a rollout is performed.

AI is going to be a major player in AEC project management, however, I recommend wading slowly into the waters of AI, as opposed to diving in headfirst.

This phase in the PM ecosystem, PM Utilities, often confuses or overwhelms organizations to the point of inaction. Follow the steps in this chapter and you will make progress in this important

---

10 "Artificial Intelligence." Merriam-Webster.com. 2025. https://www. Merrian-Webster.com (20 February 2025).

component of your ecosystem. It is my hope that you find these guidelines useful in approaching PM tools, templates, and software.

In the PM Resource Pack available for download at PMResourcePack.com you will find a list of questions you can use to survey your PMs on their current tools, as well as a list of some podcast interviews and webinars that we conducted related to AI in the AEC industry.

PHASE IV

PHASE I
PM Pillars

Project Management Office

PM Onboarding & Mentoring

PHASE IV
PM Support

PM Development

PM Utilities

CHAPTER 6

PM ONBOARDING THE RIGHT WAY

WITH THE RAPID GROWTH of AEC organizations, both organic and by acquisition, onboarding project managers (the right way) is more important than ever. Failure to do so may have a very negative impact on project success as well as client relationships.

Over the years as we have worked with firms to build PM development programs, we would often have conversations with our clients about onboarding new PMs. They would often ask questions like, "We have a new PM starting this week, can we enroll them in the next session of the PM development program that starts early next year?" We would always agree to that, but I started to ask myself, "Is it really good practice for them to wait that long to teach new PMs how to manage projects?" The answer to that question is absolutely not.

So, we started working with our clients on building better processes for onboarding new project managers, whether it was one PM, or a group of them through an acquisition. Based on what I've learned, I'd like to share five strategies that you can use to quickly onboard PMs the right way, so that they can be effective immediately.

Before we dive into these strategies, you might be wondering why onboarding is in the final phase of the PM ecosystem. I have found that it's beneficial for companies to develop some of the other components of the ecosystem which can then be used to assist in onboarding PMs.

For example, some of our clients use the session recordings from their PM development program to create PM onboarding videos. Again, you do not have to follow the phases of the ecosystem in order. Address them in the order that makes the most sense for your organization.

#1 BUILD PM ONBOARDING INTO YOUR STANDARD ONBOARDING PROCESS

Most AEC organizations have a standard onboarding process that the Human Resources team executes for all new hires. The process usually includes things like giving them their employee handbook, having them fill out forms, and setting up their payroll profile. Why not include an introduction to project management in that process?

This could be done by facilitating a short conversation with a PM in the organization or providing some literature or other content (i.e., audio or video) introducing them to how your organization manages projects. If project management is so important to the success of an AEC organization, we should discuss it from day one with a new hire. It doesn't have to be overwhelming, but highlighting project management early on will send a message that your organization has a strong project management culture.

#2 PRODUCE AN ON-DEMAND INTRODUCTION TO PROJECT MANAGEMENT COURSE

This recommendation is a step up from the last one and is something we have done successfully for many of our clients. Create a series of short videos that you can present as an "Introduction to Project Management" course. The course would serve as an orientation for new PMs; it would help them to immediately understand how your organization executes and delivers projects.

Since it is on-demand, they can do it at a time that works best for them. Developing a course like this provides two huge benefits.

Firstly, it allows new hires to take advantage of some of the downtime that is inevitable in your first few weeks at a new company. You remember when you last started a new job, you tend to be very light on things to do over the first two to four weeks while they are ramping you up. This is the perfect time for a new hire to watch videos and start to understand your PM processes. They feel productive, and the knowledge they gain will help them be a more effective PM in your ecosystem faster.

Secondly, the benefit that the on-demand course provides is that it bridges the gap from the time they start with your organization, until the time you can offer them a full PM development program. Bridging this gap gives your new PM a chance to understand how the team works, while waiting for the scheduled development opportunity.

#3 PROVIDE AN EXPERIENCED PM AS A MENTOR

I have had the opportunity to interview hundreds of AEC project managers through designing custom programs and conducting podcast interviews. Approximately 80% of them (and that is not an exaggeration) claim that the most effective development experience for them as a PM was provided by learning from a mentor.

Project managers will often cite one or two mentors that really helped them to grow their confidence as well as their PM and leadership skills. PM development programs are great for skill building, but they don't necessarily help PMs build their confidence, which is what a mentor can do. A mentor also shares wisdom from past experiences that are often hard to capture and teach in a formal course.

You might create a formal mentoring program for project managers, or simply create an onboarding mentor. For example, oftentimes in elementary schools that have grades kindergarten through six, there is a "buddy system." When kindergarteners show up on the first day of school, they are introduced to a sixth grader who will be their "buddy" for the first month of school to help them get acclimated.

Consider a buddy system of your own where new PM hires are connected with experienced PMs who can guide them through the first 30 to 90 days with your organization. It may end up being more productive than any development course!

It can also be helpful to build mentoring into your culture through servant leadership, which encourages team members to help one another. We do this at EMI, and it creates an amazing avenue for informal mentoring, which is just as valuable as formal or organized mentoring.

#4 ALLOW NEW PMs TO SERVE A DEPUTY ROLE ON THEIR FIRST PROJECT

Another strategy that can facilitate PM onboarding is to allow each new PM hire to serve as deputy PM on their first project. The dictionary defines the word deputy as *a second in command or assistant who usually takes charge when his or her superior is absent.*[11] This strategy allows the new PM to get involved in project management immediately, but not take on the full responsibility or pressure that the primary project manager assumes.

Providing the deputy role essentially creates the mentoring relationship that I discussed in the last strategy, however it combines mentoring with project management on an actual project. I consider this the best of both worlds. The new PM is getting mentoring and guidance that they can immediately put into action in real project situations. Many of our clients have had very positive experiences utilizing a deputy PM role.

#5 ENROLL NEW PMs IN YOUR LIVE PM DEVELOPMENT PROGRAM ASAP

Last, but not least, provide live training through your project management development program as soon as possible for new PM hires. As I said earlier in this chapter, this isn't always easy to do because most organizations only offer live programs once or twice per year. However, if you employ some of the first four strategies that I have described in this chapter, the lag time leading up to the live training won't be detrimental. In fact, it might be beneficial, in that they would already have a basic understanding and some mentoring on how project management is executed in your organization.

If you want to get a feel for how important project management is to an AEC organization ask them the following question, **"When you hire a PM, how long is it before you provide them with PM training?"** The answer will tell you everything you need

---

11 "Deputy." Merriam-Webster.com. 2025. https://www.Merrian-Webster. com (20 February 2025).

to know. By the way, I used the word training there because that is how most organizations refer to it, however, as mentioned earlier, personally I prefer the word "development."

My main point of this entire book is that the key to sustainable development for AEC organizations is effective project management through a PM ecosystem. Consistently great project management is hard to come by, but if your organization can achieve it, you will grow sustainably. How you onboard new PMs is one of the most important things that your firm will do, and therefore I recommend you implement as many of the strategies from this chapter as soon as possible.

CHAPTER 7

IS IT TIME FOR A PMO?
If Not Now, When?

ANOTHER QUESTION THAT **AEC** organizations often ask me is, "Should we start a PMO?" Let me start by defining a Project Management Office (PMO), which I have found through my research, isn't that easy to do since there are so many different definitions.

I did find an informative conference paper that provided this definition from the Project Management Institute. PMI defines Project Management Office as: An organizational body or entity assigned various responsibilities related to the centralized and coordinated management of those projects under its domain.[12]

My definition of a PMO in the AEC industry, strictly based on working with many firms, is: A department (which could start with just one person) responsible for overseeing all of the project

---

12 Dietrich, P., Artto, K. A., & Kujala, J. (2010). Strategic priorities and PMO functions in project-based firms. Paper presented at PMI® Research Conference: Defining the Future of Project Management, Washington, DC. Newtown Square, PA: Project Management Institute.

management efforts including tools, templates, and software utilized companywide.

Please note, in this chapter I will not be addressing *how* to build a PMO, but rather identify *when* you should build one, and which type to build. I am only going to provide a high-level outline of the steps that your organization can take in this process. If you would like to dive in deeper on this topic, there are several books and other sources of information available that focus solely on PMOs.

STEP #1—IDENTIFY THE NEED AND SET THE VISION

The first step in establishing a PMO is recognizing that you need one. Unfortunately, there isn't an engineering equation to help you to do this. I have found that most firms realize that they need a PMO when they start to see a lack of consistency across their organization's PM efforts, which often results in poor quality project deliverables, which can lead to multiple problems, one of them being lawsuits.

If you are noticing that consistency is lacking and different PMs across your organization are managing projects differently, using different tools, and getting different results, then a PMO may be the answer. Should you make this realization, you will then need to set a clear objective for the PMO, which is likely tied to the type of PMO you decide to create.

In an article entitled Which PMO is Right for Your Organization, The Project Management Institute cites six different types of PMOs.[13] The article cites the following:

1. **Enterprise Project Management Office (EPMO):**
   An EPMO creates standards, processes, and delivery approaches to improve project performance across

---

13   Project Management Institute. Which PMO Is Right for Your Organization? (2023).

the organization—and typically is the go-to authority for allocating resources to different projects. Designed to operate at the corporate level, EPMOs hold maximum strategic influence and ensure that projects are aligned with organizational objectives and priorities. EPMOs are typically utilized in large organizations to ensure companywide cohesion.

2. **Departmental PMO:** A departmental PMO supports multiple projects at a department or business unit level. Its primary role is to integrate initiatives of different sizes within a division, such as IT or finance—from small, short-term initiatives to multiyear programs with multiple resources and complex integration of technologies. In keeping with its name, this type of PMO is utilized within a department.

3. **Individual PMO:** This type of PMO is designed to develop a framework for infrastructure, document management, and training for a single complex project or program. Individual PMOs set basic standards and oversee planning and control activities for a single project.

4. **Supportive PMO:** By leaning on internal experts, a supportive PMO provides consultative assistance to projects by supplying templates, good practices, training, access to information, and lessons learned from other projects. This type of PMO acts almost like a project management customer service line that

PMs within an organization can call when help is needed. It is more reactive than proactive, but could be a good approach for smaller firms when initiating a PMO.

5. **Controlling PMO:** This type of PMO is designed to provide more control by facilitating compliance. The objective for this type of PMO is to adopt project management frameworks or approaches and designate specific templates, forms, and tools. With a top-down structure, it might conduct regular audits and require project teams to follow rigid processes—think "PMO police." This format is one that I have seen in many of our AEC client organizations and can be effective in that just the threat of a PM audit can keep your PMs on their toes.

6. **Project Management Community of Practice/ Excellence:** This one is an alternative or almost a baby step towards a PMO. Establishing such a working group (also known as a center of excellence) within an organization can help seed a project management framework and establish a consensus for basic tools, templates, and approaches.

If you don't have a PMO at all, you should probably start with a PM Community of Practice (CoP) and work backwards through PMI's list of options as your company grows. This first step is more about identifying that you need a PMO and starting to brainstorm on which type, however, you do not need to select the exact type just yet, you can do that during step four of this process.

STEP #2—SEEK BUY-IN AT THE EXECUTIVE LEVEL

Any big initiative in an AEC firm requires buy-in and approval from senior leadership and a PMO is no different. Most of our clients that decide to start a PMO either do so by promoting someone internally to oversee the PMO or hiring someone, both of which typically require approval from senior management.

To obtain this buy-in and approval, you will need to show leadership the value of the PMO and provide budgeting and financial information that will support your case. One way to do this is to examine your project write-offs or write-downs from previous years. If a PMO can reduce those write-offs by a certain amount of dollars, that is a great return-on-investment to cite. You might also consider that a PMO can save your project managers time on some of the busy-work, like creating templates and organizing project files, which can help them to maintain a higher utilization, positively affecting the company's bottom line.

One of our clients, a large private AEC firm, partnered with us to develop a custom PM program and secured approval by demonstrating that the skills learned from the program would help project managers complete their projects more efficiently and provide a potential $1 million return-on-investment through reduced annual write-offs.

STEP #3—EVALUATE YOUR CURRENT PM STANDARDS

It's important to thoroughly evaluate where your organization is today with respect to PM processes, tools, and capabilities. This should be done early in the process. I mentioned this earlier when I talked about creating a project management development strategy, however when investing in building a PMO, everything needs to be done in even more detail as the investment may be greater.

Be sure to evaluate your current practices across all departments of the organization and identify gaps and areas for improvement that the PMO can remedy. This step should include conversations with PMs across your organization. You could also consider utilizing a formal assessment to gather data like I discussed in Chapter 2.

For example, if you are seeing scope creep happen companywide, one of the first initiatives of the PMO might be to improve the scoping development and monitoring processes companywide.

The result of this step should be a clear picture of where your organization performs best related to project management, and where improvements are most needed. This information will allow you to better define the structure of your PMO throughout the next steps.

STEP #4—DEFINE PMO TYPE, STRUCTURE, AND ROLES

Now that you have identified the need for a PMO, you have buy-in from leadership, and you have assessed your PM practices companywide, it's time to decide on the type and organizational structure of the PMO.

Revisit step one in this process and select the type of PMO that best supports your current needs. As I mentioned earlier, if your organization is small to mid-sized, you might start with a PM Community of Practice (CoP) or Center of Excellence. Whichever type you choose to employ, you should outline the hierarchy of the PMO. Will it be headed by a PMO Director? Will it consist of all project managers across the organization? Essentially, you are creating an organizational chart for the PMO.

Part of this step would be to define the roles and responsibilities of each PMO member, and most importantly, decide on the reporting structure. This last piece is important, because it dictates whether the PMO is a standalone unit within the organization or a secondary unit. When I say secondary unit, I mean, all PMs may work primarily in their technical divisions (i.e., structures, roadway, stormwater, etc.) but by default they are members of the PMO as well by title. This goes back to the PM identity crisis I discussed in Chapter 1, where companies struggle to figure out how to classify their PMs. This process may help you to decide.

STEP #5—CREATE THE PMO GUIDELINES AND GOVERNANCE

The first thing we do when we work with a client to build a PM development program is to determine what the typical project life-cycle looks like within their organization.

The Project Management Institute (PMI) defines a project's lifecycle as five phases:[14]

- **Initiating:** Define the project's goals, constraints, and budget

- **Planning:** Create a plan to achieve the project's goals

- **Executing:** Put the plan into action

- **Monitoring and Controlling:** Track progress and adjust

- **Closing:** Bring the project to completion and document it

While this is a nice outline, you must further define each of these phases in your project lifecycle and customize it to the type of projects that your organization executes.

---

14 Project Management Institute. (2021). A Guide to the Project Management Body of Knowledge (PMBOK® Guide)---Seventh Edition. Newtown Square, PA: Project Management Institute.

This lifecycle will serve as a roadmap for success for your PMO and your project managers in general. It gives them a path to follow for each project. Then the PMO can develop guidelines, tools, and standards for each of the phases and sub-phases throughout the lifecycle.

During this step you should consider what high level PM approaches your organization will employ (i.e., Agile, Hybrid, etc.), and governance policies you wish to implement (risk management, compliance, work at risk, etc.).

STEP #6—DECIDE ON AND CREATE PMO TOOLS AND TEMPLATES

I have already spent an entire chapter on this topic, but it is a critical step in the development of a PMO. You must make important decisions including what type of PM software is best for your organization as well as the tools and templates that will be needed. By creating a typical project life cycle for your organization, you can align these tools and templates with each phase within the lifecycle. For example, in the planning phase, you would provide a template for a project management plan (PMP). This makes it easier for your PMs to focus on managing projects, not creating, or trying to find the right tools to do so.

When selecting a software be sure it is comprehensive enough for your projects, but not overly complicated that your PMs won't use it. It is important that they can easily generate reports that will show them the right information with regard to the status of their projects regarding both schedule and cost.

Part of this step should also be to consider what key performance indicators (KPIs) your PMs will be assessed on. Essentially, in this step you are deciding on the key metrics to determine the success of your projects and project managers, and how you will help them measure those metrics.

STEP #7—LAUNCH AND GROW YOUR PMO

Now it's time to launch your PMO. I recommend starting with a small-scale pilot phase before you implement it companywide. This is a big undertaking and approaching it with a *walk first, then run* approach is a good starting point.

Collect a lot of feedback during the pilot phase and refine your processes. Then as the PMO takes flight, you can expand it across the organization.

TWO FINAL THOUGHTS ON PMOs

There are two last points I want to make about PMOs. Similar to each and every human being, your PMO will never be "finished" it will always be a work in progress, just like we all are. So, don't think of pushing it across the finish line. It is not a project that you can complete, it's more of an ongoing process of being able to foster effective project management across your organization.

Lastly, most PMOs require one person to really start it and walk through the steps outlined in this chapter. Typically, this is a person with a good amount of diverse project management experience. Someone who is ready for the next step in their career. Maybe they are ready to graduate from managing projects to helping all of your PMs manage their projects better.

This person should have good interpersonal and leadership skills since they will have to interact with PMs across your organization. Their communication skills should be above average, and they should be someone that you trust to invest heavily in their development.

The reason this component is found in Phase IV of the PM ecosystem is because most firms begin building a PMO once the firm is large enough to support it. Starting a PMO can be a lengthy process, but also one of the most important things that an AEC organization can focus on to drive sustainable growth.

Now that we've addressed all four phases of your PM ecosystem, I'd like to walk through how to build and continually develop it in the final two chapters.

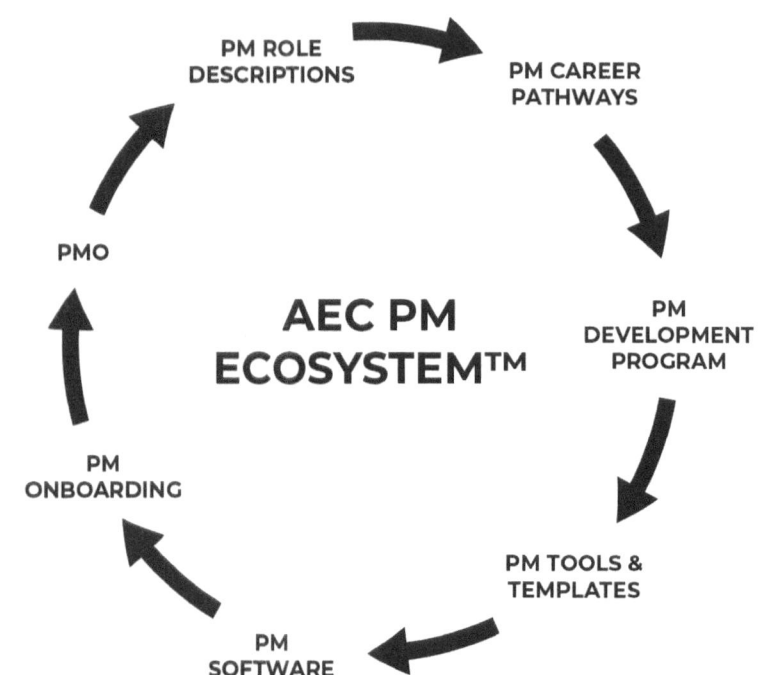

PM ROLE
DESCRIPTIONS

PM CAREER
PATHWAYS

PMO

AEC PM
ECOSYSTEM™

PM
DEVELOPMENT
PROGRAM

PM
ONBOARDING

PM
SOFTWARE

PM TOOLS &
TEMPLATES

CHAPTER 8

BUILD YOUR PM ECOSYSTEM TO CREATE SUSTAINABLE GROWTH

THE MISTAKE OF MOST firms is to offer a few disjointed training efforts for their PMs without developing the other components of a healthy PM ecosystem. This is the way we now discuss project management to our AEC clients; we frame out everything I have detailed in this book as an AEC PM Ecosystem™. You now have the information you need to build yours.

In this chapter, I am going to provide a recap of the components of the AEC PM Ecosystem™ that I have detailed through this book as a call to action to inspire you to start building yours today.

If you can build 50% of the following ecosystem components, you will be ahead of most AEC organizations.

PM JOB TITLES AND ROLE DESCRIPTIONS

Start by ensuring you have clear titles and roles for your project managers. Are they solely managing projects, or responsible for project management amongst other things? Consider various levels of project manager like Junior PM, Deputy PM, PM, and Senior PM. This will allow you to really think through the progression of the project manager position in your organization. The questions in Chapter 1 can serve as guidance in developing this component of your ecosystem.

PM CAREER PROGRESSION INCLUDING CAREER PATHWAYS

Once you have your PM titles and role descriptions you can chart them out in a career progression or career path. You can attempt to define each level of the career progression by creating a description or list of requirements for each one. For example, many of our clients will require their professionals to achieve our AEC PM Essentials Certification, which demonstrates an understanding of foundational PM concepts, before officially being named a Project Manager. Then later in their career progression they are required to achieve our AEC PM Advanced Certification, which demonstrates an understanding of more advanced PM concepts. These certifications ensure that they have completed courses with practical assignments on relevant topics. You could do something similar with your internal development programs.

PM ASSESSMENT

The key to developing strong PMs is understanding their individual strengths and needs instead of applying a one-size-fits-all approach. Firms can do this through surveys, industry assessments like the AEC PM Behaviors Assessment, and direct conversations with PMs across different experience levels. Collecting this data helps create a targeted development strategy that actually prepares PMs for success. Formal assessments provide insight into key skills, while interviews can reveal gaps in training and consistency across teams. With the right approach, firms can ensure their PM training is relevant, effective, and actually helps their teams grow. Remember, not all PMs are created equal!

PM DEVELOPMENT PROGRAM

It is critical that you provide practical, transferable learning and development opportunities to your project managers, not just training or bootcamps. Build a program around the PM career progression that you created if possible.

Depending on the size of your organization, you might use external learning and development organizations like EMI to deliver your programs and certify your PMs. That is still part of your PM ecosystem. Whatever PM development programs you decide to utilize, internal or external, ensure that they align with the other components of your ecosystem.

PM TOOLS AND TEMPLATES

Your development program will educate your PMs on important project management skills. However, it is still recommended that you provide PM tools and templates to help them effectively execute their projects. Failure to do this could result in a lack of consistency in project delivery across your organization. If every office is using a different tool for resourcing, or a different spreadsheet for estimating, your ecosystem won't be as aligned as it should be.

As I mentioned in Chapter 5, while it is important to create a standard set of tools and templates, it is also good to provide flexibility in understanding that different clients and project types might pose different requirements. Resources like the AEC PM Toolkit which offers a library of standard tools and templates provides a good starting point that you can further develop. You can find information about the toolkit at PMResourcePack.com.

PM SOFTWARE

Decide on which type of PM software you want to use and implement it across your organization. This is always one of the most difficult components of the ecosystem because it can be a very complex initiative.

Again, I won't go into a lot of detail here, but I can tell you from what I have learned that **simple is often better**. Set up your software and figure out the key components and reports that will be most helpful for your PMs and train them on only those. Take it one step at a time or they will get overwhelmed, and they won't use it.

PM ONBOARDING

Once you have these key components in place, and remember it will always be a work in progress, then you should create a world class PM Onboarding process.

With your AEC PM Ecosystem™ in place, onboarding should be a lot easier. You'll have clear PM titles and roles and a career pathway for PMs to follow. The key to successful PM onboarding is ensuring that you can immediately introduce them to your company's "way" of managing projects. In Chapter 6, I give you some examples of how to do this, the best one being an introductory "do it yourself" video course that new PMs can use to get acclimated until you can enroll them in your PM development program.

PROJECT MANAGEMENT OFFICE (PMO)

At a certain size, your organization might create a PMO that will be responsible for nurturing your PM ecosystem. Chapter 7 takes you through the process of deciding on when to start a PMO and which type might be best for your organization. Most of our AEC client firms start with a PM Community of Practice (CoP) and grow from there.

CHAPTER 9

CONTINUOUS DEVELOPMENT ALWAYS

O NE OF THE MOST important concepts to grasp when build-ing your PM ecosystem, including the development of your PMs, is that **the process will never end.**

Change will always occur, whether that be changes within your organization, like growth, changes in the industry, economy, or other changes. All these factors will likely impact how your organization manages and delivers projects.

This is a very important thing to remember and a mindset to cultivate. You should constantly remind yourself and others that your PM ecosystem and all of its components are a work in progress. If you or your colleagues, including your PMO Director, is striving to finish, they will likely burnout because it is highly unlikely that project management in your organization will ever be "finished."

In this chapter, I want to offer up five actions that your organization can take to continuously develop your project managers, the processes that they use to do their jobs, and the entire PM ecosystem. These can be applied individually or organizationally depending on your role or situation.

#1—ALWAYS EXPAND YOUR TEAM'S PROJECT MANAGEMENT KNOWLEDGE

Project management is a rapidly changing field. We are learning more about different PM philosophies (i.e., Agile) every day. There are also many new tools available, in large part due to AI, that can help your PMs streamline their efforts.

Look for ways to ensure that your project managers are staying up to date on industry trends and best practices. You can encourage your PMs to join industry groups or seek certifications like the AEC PM, both which can serve as ways to build their PM knowledge and network. At EMI, we provide our quarterly PM Assist™ Live webinars, for all AEC PM certification holders, featuring industry experts discussing relevant PM topics.

In the PM Resource Pack available for download at PMResourcePack.com you can find a link to a recording of one of our PM Assist Live webinars titled AI in Project Management.

#2—KEEP YOUR PMs TECHNICAL SKILLS SHARP

Often in the AEC industry, when a professional becomes a PM, they work on less of the technical details and more on the management aspects of projects. This is good! This is what we want them to do. However, they should not become so far removed from the technical side of projects to the point where it reduces their ability to effectively lead their project teams and be knowledgeable in front of project stakeholders.

You must strive to ensure that your PMs maintain enough technical knowledge to effectively manage their teams and ensure they have the right team members working on the right tasks. Their technical knowledge will also ensure that they can oversee or help when needed on basic PM tasks like creating the right work breakdown structure or project schedule. Their team members will respect them if they are able to speak the same (technical) language as them.

#3—DEVELOP COMMUNICATION AND LEADERSHIP SKILLS FOR EVERYONE

I can't stress this point enough. Your projects will not be executed efficiently if your PMs AND their team members can't communicate effectively, AND lead others.

You MUST find ways to consistently improve communication and leadership skills across your organization. One way to do this is to consider creating internal communications or public speaking courses.

I have seen many AEC firms build Toastmasters chapters within their organizations. Toastmasters International is a non-profit educational organization that helps individuals improve their public speaking, communication, and leadership skills. It operates through a network of local clubs worldwide, where members practice speaking, receive feedback, and develop confidence in a supportive environment.

You might also challenge your PMs and others to present more, whether it be at client or project meetings, or internal staff meetings. This will build their confidence and ultimately their communication and leadership skills. If opportunities for your PMs to practice their speaking skills are slim, Toastmasters can be an invaluable tool.

I recommend putting an emphasis on developing people leadership skills for PMs. Many of the AEC firms we work with initially are looking to just teach their PMs the hard skills like managing scopes, schedules, and budgets. However, we urge them to integrate people leadership skills (i.e., communication, conversation skills, active listening, negotiating, etc.) into their development programs. Project managers need many different skills to be successful.

Do whatever it takes to ensure that your organization prioritizes the development of these two skill sets, communication and leadership. In all my work with AEC firms, I would say this area is the most undervalued and can lead to the largest return-on-investment for an organization.

#4—PROVIDE HANDS-ON EXPERIENCE FOR YOUR PMs AS SOON AS POSSIBLE

By now you know I am a huge proponent of formal development programs for project managers, however just as important, is allowing them to build their skills through hands-on experience.

As a newer consulting engineer, I was thrown into the fire of project management at a young age when an experienced PM left the firm I worked for. While this experience was painful at times, because I felt that my PM skills were inadequate, the experience ultimately helped me to build strong PM skills through experience. Yes, I made mistakes, but I learned from them, and it made me a better PM very early in my career.

Look for ways to involve your PMs or future PMs in project management activities as early as possible in their careers. I believe that if you wait until they are "ready," you are doing a disservice to them because you are not allowing for on-the-job development, which many PMs have told me was the most valuable learning experience they had in their careers.

One way to do this, which I mentioned earlier, is to allow soon-to-be or new PMs to shadow more experienced PMs on projects and pitch in where they can. This will start the PM skill development process early on.

#5—ENCOURAGE YOUR PMs TO NETWORK AMONGST OTHER PROJECT MANAGERS

This final action may require some prodding and persuading on your end, but it will be worth it. Encourage your project managers to get involved in the PM community, whether that be through joining a local PMI chapter or attending industry conferences, webinars, or in-person events like EMI's AEC PM Connect™.

These networking activities provide multiple benefits. They will help build their confidence and communication skills, and they will allow them to stay up to date on trending PM topics through these networking efforts. Your PMs are going to have to interact with people outside of your organization to ensure they are obtaining important industry information and bring it back to your larger PM population.

We started the AEC PM Connect™ events because our clients kept asking me, "What are your other AEC clients doing when it comes to project management?" I now answer, "Come to AEC PM Connect™ and ask them!"

Never assume that your company knows everything they need to know about project management. This assumption will absolutely prevent continuous development.

Please consider promoting as many of these actions as you can with your project managers. When it comes to your organization's PM skills, remember this quote from the late author William S. Burroughs, "When you stop growing, you start dying."[15]

---

15 "When you stop growing, you start dying." Goodreads.com. 2025. https://www.goodreads.com/quotes/314286-when-you-stop-growing-you-start-dying (21 March 2025).

YOU ARE NOW READY TO BUILD YOUR SCALABLE PROJECT MANAGEMENT ECOSYSTEM

I hope you found the information in this book insightful and useful. My goal is that you can take what you've learned and apply it within your organization to build a thriving AEC PM Ecosystem™ and, in turn, world class project management efforts, which I believe is the key to rapid, sustainable growth for AEC organizations.

You now have the framework you need to achieve sustainable growth for years to come. There will be challenges along the way, but if you commit to it, and follow the framework that this book provides, you can find great success like the many firms I have mentioned.

I wish you the best on your quest to build a scalable PM ecosystem that drives sustainable growth for your organization for years to come.

ACKNOWLEDGMENTS

This book would not have been possible without the keen editorial eye of Ella Rice, whose insights made this book easier to read and apply.

Thank you to James Woosley of Free Agent Press for helping to pull this book together in a short period of time, a great project management feat in itself.

To my family who continues to allow me to chase my crazy dreams and ideas, I am grateful for each of you.

To all my team members at the Engineering Management Institute, by adopting our values of Give, Guide, and Grow, and living them out every day, you have inspired me and others. This book is another avenue for us to help AEC professionals become better project managers and leaders, both at work and at home. I am grateful to every member of the EMI team for their unwavering support. A special thanks to our learning & development team leaders Betty, Ana, Fiona, and Michelle, who inspired many of the ideas in this book and gave feedback through the writing process. Also, a special thanks to Elloise for creating the AEC PM Ecosystem™ image.

To all the engineers and other professionals out there that have read, listened to, or watched EMI's content over the years and have shared positive messages with me about how our content has helped them grow-thank you! Your messages have been inspiring, and I have shared them with our content team at EMI, who, led by our fearless Content Team Leader, Angelique, has done tireless work ensuring that the content guides professionals globally.

Writing this book has further cemented my decision to leave my engineering career behind years ago to focus more on helping technical professionals grow. It is rewarding beyond belief.

The most important equation that I have learned in life is Give + Guide = Growth, and my goal is that this book will unlock more growth in AEC project managers and their organizations.

LIST OF IMAGES

Figure 1: PM Success Cycle (Engineering Management Institute, 2025)

Figure 2: Five Process Groups (Project Management Institute, 2025)

Figure 3: AEC PM Ecosystem™ (Engineering Management Institute, 2025)

Figure 4: *The Six Disciplines of Breakthrough Learning* (Pollock, Mck. Jefferson, Wick, 2015)

Figure 5: SWOT Quadrants Sample (Engineering Management Institute, 2025)

Figure 6: 80/20 Chart (*Living the 80/20 Way*, Koch, 2014)

EngineeringManagementInstitute.org

www.ingramcontent.com/pod-product-compliance
Lightning Source LLC
Chambersburg PA
CBHW031436120626
46545CB00006B/2441